"I do believe something magical
can happen when you read
a good book"

-J.K. Rowling

Author of the Harry Potter book series

This book
is a gift

To

From

Enjoy and Share

Praise for *Finding your Hummus*
by Michael Kouly

"Finding Your Hummus is a WONDERFUL recipe book for life Read it and learn to enjoy the experience of living!"

Marshall Goldsmith – The Thinkers 50 #1
Leadership Thinker in the World and author of
the #1 New York Times bestseller – Triggers

"Michael Kouly has written a marvelous text on how to live a life with purpose. Captured in this fascinating parable are gems of wisdom that come from a writer who has deep insight into human nature and what is required to grow, contribute and find an abiding sense of fulfillment."

Dean Williams, Director, The Global Change
Agent program, Harvard Kennedy School

"Finding your hummus is a lovely book of spiritual awakening that I am reading to my baby son. I will continue to read it to him as he grows older in order to instill in him optimism and moral courage. The stories are simple and full of meaning and they inspire hope over adversity. The relationship between the three struggling siblings Sara, Adam and Tom reflects a family committed to love and the struggle to overcome disappointments and to loving toil, essentially Freud's life-goals. The language is beautiful and the drawings superb."

Trevor Mostyn, Author and Educator, Oxford Univeristy

This story can transform you
and your company

FINDING
YOUR
HUMMUS

Discover your personal
and organizational purpose

MICHAEL KOULY

First Edition

ISBN 978-0-9992181-0-5

This book is dedicated to my daughter Maria-Helena, son Paul-Anthony and wife Sandra, and through them to all families, professionals, businesspeople, entrepreneurs and public officials who are seeking meaning that gives depth to their journey in this amazing experience that we call life.

Acknowledgments

This book was written in its first basic form in about two weeks in early 2015, but it took two years and the help of good people to bring it to its current form. I would like to particularly acknowledge the precious contribution that my colleagues at Cambridge Institute for Global Leadership (CIGL) and Kouly Institute, Marwa Itani and Najwa Ghotmi, made in reviewing, enriching, adding content, editing, and most importantly making the entire journey from first draft to publishing so much fun.

I also recognize the significant contribution that my colleague Mary Shammas made by creating the illustrations that were each drawn by her talented hands. Mary is also the designer of the cover page and is the one who formatted the content into a publishable form on paper and electronically.

In addition, I would like to mention Jim Crupi, Kate Queen, Jo Lavender, and Devika Brendon whose contributions deserve special thanks.

It would take many more paragraphs to mention each person, across five continents, who reviewed, edited, and gave feedback on the book. The same applies to all people who have been encouraging me to write, with the help of colleagues at CIGL and Kouly Institute, this book and the other books that will follow on the subjects of leadership, strategy, purpose, authority, and fulfillment. To each of them I say THANK YOU; every word and gesture of encouragement you made had, and continues to have, a significant impact on our research, publishing, teaching and advisory activities that we do worldwide.

I have Found my Hummus, that has led me to write Finding Your Hummus. I hope you Find your Hummus as well, very soon, and discover how delicious life can be.

Shift Happens!

I leave it to you to decide whether or not this story actually happened, or could happen!

This story is meant to be enjoyed by people of various ages and backgrounds and, no offense is meant to you, beautiful reader, especially by my soon-to-be teenage daughter Maria, and later by my six-year- young son Paul-Anthony, when he is able to read it.

This story can be read as a metaphorical perspective on personal, familial and business matters of life. This story is my story. This story is your story. It is up to your imagination to take it as far and as deep as you want to go.

Shift Happens Even to the Bests!

Once upon a time, there was a family living in a faraway land called SOMELAND. It was a small tight-knit community where everybody knew your name and nobody forgot your missteps so people were careful to make few. Secrets couldn't be kept for long and privacy was an unusual concept. Children wanted to play outside and their parents let them. Technological gadgets and cars were not often used in SOMELAND.

The land was filled with farms and coal mines. Horses and donkeys were the choices of transport, and if you had something to say to your neighbor, the best form of communication was a good old-fashioned visit. Although the people had their differences, in the end, they treated one another like family.

The Bests were a typical family of SOMELAND. Father worked long hours in the coal mines, but never so long that he didn't have the time, energy, or love to enjoy his three wonderful children. He told long stories about beautiful princesses, terrifying dragons, and brave knights by the fire at night. They lasted for hours, sometimes even for days, but even then, they seemed too short to his eager audience. Father's eyes would light up and his hands would come alive with gestures, lending nuance and action to his words. His family would gather around him, listening and sharing the world he drew in the empty air.

Mother farmed the lands. She raised chickpeas and children, neither of which grew too fast. She was silly, and laughed in the way happy people laugh, deep from her soul.

Tom, the eldest child, was the only one to finish his education, and began building houses. He made a name for himself in the community and was known for his signature home designs. Nobody saw buildings the way Tom did: he turned bricks into art, innovated and explored, and built real homes, not just houses. He even found the love of his life in SOMELAND. She was everything one could hope for in a future wife in SOMELAND: beautiful, kind, and content.

Adam was the middle child; he was quiet, shy, and preferred to keep to himself. He loved to watch things grow and change, he loved the way the seed split and twisted itself into a stem and leaves, and he loved the way autumn shifted all colors to gold.

Sara was the youngest of three, daddy's little girl, and always creating and crafting with her nimble fingers. She wanted to be like the princesses in her daddy's stories, so it was never surprising when she brought home a frog to kiss, or a few mice to help her sew a dress. She loved learning and exploring, whether it was sitting at a desk, swinging from a tree, or lying at Father's feet to absorb his words. She loved to create and imagine, and his stories were the magical thread weaving her life together.

But sometimes in SOMELAND, things do not go as planned...

Father fell ill with latiposis, a rare and serious disease. He couldn't work or care for himself, let alone for his family. He grew weaker quickly, unable to rise from his bed, or even feed himself. Mother spent hours at his bedside, instead of in the fields, and weeds ran rampant over their crops, throttling them.

Money became tight, and Adam was forced to leave high school to help at home, but every cloud has a silver lining. As he helped his mother keep the farm under control, tend to his father, and make meals, he realized his true passion in life. The crackle of oil in a pan, the "che-chunk" of a knife through a vegetable, the steam of roasting – they lightened his heart, even on days when Father was very ill, and Mother shut herself in the bedroom with him for hours.

It didn't take long for Adam to start experimenting, to try mixing different ingredients to see what worked and what didn't – and sometimes the strangest things brought out the best flavors. Adam read every cookery book in the house, and his creativity bloomed from their pages into the most wonderful shapes and tastes. He always carried around a notebook to jot down little notes for his recipes, but found that through cooking he often learned more about life than he had ever learned from a book. Just like the recipes which he hoped would be passed down through his family, he wrote those lessons down too.

Sara stayed in school because she was still too young to be much help around the house. Nights were hard for her because her haven that was once filled with her father's stories was now filled only with silence. She remembered the stories vividly and could conjure them into pictures in her head. She took to painting these pictures, charcoaling and inking and coloring paper to remember all the wonderful tales her Father had told her, and to drive back the silence that filled her head otherwise.

Tom worked enthusiastically day and night to help with the finances. He was proud of his remarkable success, and happy to contribute when the family needed him most. Not everyone gets to leave their mark on the world, but to the ones they hold dear, their efforts will never be forgotten.

The situation, however, kept getting worse. Then one day, Mother received a tip from a neighbor that over in a place called ANYLAND, her husband could be cured of his disease. Mother spent days thinking it over, until, finally, she felt that the family had no other choice but to leave. The children didn't take the news too well, especially Tom, who was settled and happy in SOMELAND. He had met the perfect future wife for SOMELAND, but not for ANYLAND. She did not wish to leave, for she was content, and found changing life partners to be easier than changing life plans. At first, Tom considered staying, but as he was the eldest and the only one with work experience, he felt he needed to help his family out. He was driven by his sense of responsibility.

They only had a few days to say their goodbyes.

On the last day, all the neighbors gathered to bid their farewells and offered some money to help with the long journey ahead. The family decided to pass their land over to their quirky neighbor, Hank, who was a mentor to Adam. Hank had often helped them with the farm, and he had taught Adam his love for fresh food from the earth. As Adam was saying his farewell, Hank slipped a small pouch in his hand, and whispered, "Always stay true to yourself."

Recipe Book

Be prepared; life is always changing and sometimes hard...!

Shift happens

The family traveled by bus, making many stops along the way. Father's health was not improving with the bumpy roads and uncomfortable seats, and sometimes they had to rest for a day or two before he was fit to continue. During that time, all of the money that they had received from the neighbors was used up. The only thing left was Tom's savings.

Upon arriving in ANYLAND, the family was astonished. The world they now saw around them was nothing like the one they had known. The streets were bustling with people and modern cars. Huge electronic billboards lit commercial squares. Shops were crowded, and the country seemed to offer opportunities for everyone who worked hard. There was a certain hunger in the air. The children saw their first homeless man on the ground, begging for food. Life was fast-paced and it seemed time was the most precious resource of all. People dared not waste it socializing.

"Wow!" Adam said, "I've never seen such tall buildings! Look, Tom, at how extraordinary they are. Nothing at home is built like that."

Tom looked around at the buildings, a frown coming to his face. "ANYLAND is nothing like home. Is this place really somewhere we could

live? Look at the strange buildings, the people rushing back and forth, with no time for the sunshine or the rain. This is not home."

Mother reassured them by saying, "Home isn't about the place, it's about family, and our family must make this place a home for a time. Remember that with each other, we are always home, and we will always have enough."

When they first moved in, nobody came to welcome them to the building. The landlord was a stinky man, who communicated through grunts and hand gestures symbolizing 'pay now.' The family only had a few months' worth of rent money and payment for Father's treatment, so it was necessary that they find jobs quickly. But things seemed to keep getting worse.

Their mother didn't stay with them, but at the hospital, to watch over her husband's treatment, and to offer her own in the form of affection and attention. To leave him alone in the strip lights and strange-smelling corridors of the hospital was impossible. It comforted all of them, including the children, to know that Mother and Father were facing the hospital's clinical strangeness together.

Tom's first impression of ANYLAND did not

improve. He was angry, resentful, and powerless. He missed his fiancé and old life in SOMELAND.

Sara was afraid to begin with, wanting nothing to do with the outside world. She sat by the window with her sketchbook and drew pictures of characters from her father's stories. However, as time passed, the things she could see beyond the pane of glass began to creep into her drawings – the strange buildings, the gray clouds, the street lights. Then she ventured out to find new subjects, to expand her understanding of the things she saw, and began to find friendships. By the time she started school, she thought of ANYLAND before she thought of SOMELAND, and walking home among the tall signs, along orderly streets, no longer made her feel sad or homesick.

Adam, however, had none of her carefree youth. He felt stressed and purposeless, aware that they needed income, but with no idea how to make it. Here, amongst the concrete and bricks, there were no plants for him to tend and watch, and he felt robbed of everything which he knew.

ANYLAND was different to SOMELAND; it took time to settle down, and it wasn't easy for any of them. The people, the language, the place: it was all new to them. Tom and Adam went out daily searching for work, but without success. The competition was fierce, and their hope was fading.

"I'm tired of looking for a job," said Tom. "I had a job, and a very good one."

"We're running out of savings and very soon there will be no money left to pay the rent, to buy food, and pay the hospital bills," replied Adam. "ANYLAND is booming. I'm sure there are many opportunities: we just need to keep looking and we're bound to find something eventually."

Recipe Book
Easy is not an option in life.

Relationships are complicated and are loaded with obligations.

"What opportunities?" asked Tom. "We're strangers here and we don't speak the language well. Besides, you're a farmer; so who is going to hire you in a city where there are no farming spaces? You're obsolete here, and there's nothing you can do."

"We must do this for Father." Adam shook his head firmly, ending all back and forth.

Adam didn't want to give up. He knew there had to be a way to solve this. In desperation, he knocked on his neighbors' doors, thinking perhaps they knew of job opportunities. Most sent him away, shaking their heads, and many didn't answer. Finally, one was opened by a little boy, not more than seven years old.

"Hi there," said Adam.

"Hello," replied the boy, putting his hands behind his back and looking up at him.

"Are your parents home?" Adam bent down to the boy's level.

"No, they are at work. Who are you?"

"I'm your new neighbor. I was looking for a job and thought your parents might know of a place that is hiring."

The boy didn't seem to be interested when he heard the word 'job'; he seemed to have something he considered far more important on his mind. "Hey – can you fly?" he asked eagerly.

Recipe Book

Keep a child's fresh perspective on life. Remember when life was simple and you had beautiful dreams, and you were curious and fearless.

Adam, confused by the random question, shook his head. "No."

"But why not? It's easy!" he said, with eyes wide open. "Do you want to learn?"

Adam shook his head. "I'm sorry, not today. Maybe another time."

Disappointed, the boy looked down at the floor.

"Okay, another time then."

One day, Adam and Tom came across a construction site where a house was being built.

Tom's eyes lit up at the sight of the bricks and cement-mixers, and he rushed across the street, dodging cars, to speak to the supervisor.

"Excuse me, Sir, do you need help?"

The supervisor looked at Tom and said, "What can you do for us?"

"I've been working in the field of construction for years." Tom puffed up his chest and smiled. "I'm well known for my designs."

"Well," replied the supervisor, "we don't need to design the house. We just need someone to move the piles of stone so we can get the walls up."

Tom frowned, enthusiasm vanishing. His eyes

narrowed with annoyance and arrogance.

"You expect ME to move stones? I'm a designer, not a common laborer."

"And you are?" asked the supervisor.

Standing up straight with his chin held high, Tom said, "I am Tom Best."

"Well, Mr. Best, if you have a problem with moving stones, you can move on," said the supervisor sarcastically. "We all have mouths to feed."

Adam, not wanting to waste a chance to get some work, quickly intervened. "I can move the piles of stone, Sir!"

The supervisor looked at Adam's forced smile and said, "Fine, YOU start tomorrow. You'll get 10 dollars a day."

Seeing Tom's hands shaking with annoyance, Adam quickly thanked the supervisor. "Okay, have a good day, Sir. See you tomorrow...bye," he said, as he pulled Tom away.

Although the money was barely enough to buy food for a day and he would learn quickly where the phrase "hard labor" stemmed from, Adam felt proud that he had at least got something to help his family. It's not going to be easy, he thought, but at least it's a start.

Adam would wake up early every day and go to work, where he would carry one heavy stone at a time across the large construction site. In the evening, he would collect 10 dollars from the supervisor and buy food for the family.

Recipe Book
People are instinctively
driven to survive and grow.

You must remain
intelligently adaptive,
otherwise you will perish!

"This is crazy," said Tom. "We barely have enough to eat... It would be better to go back to SOMELAND. We know the place and the language, we would live like we used to, which was certainly far better than the way we are living now."

"You forget why we are here. It's not to prosper. It's to help Father. What will we do with him in SOMELAND?" Adam asked.

"We can figure it out when we get there," replied Tom, but even as he spoke, he knew it wasn't really an option, and he let the subject go.

Recipe Book
You cannot build a better new reality with an outdated mindset.

Tom had stopped searching for work. He gave up after being told that to become a licensed builder in ANYLAND he had to go back to university and study more. The knowledge and skills required for building the standard tall towers in ANYLAND were different from those needed to design unique houses in SOMELAND. He felt it was truly unfair and yearned for the life he had had in SOMELAND. In his opinion, he had already perfected his craft, and he refused to start learning again.

One day, while Adam was moving rocks at work, a tall and physically stronger man came to the construction site.

"Do you need help, Sir?" he asked the supervisor.

"No, thank you. We have enough workers," the supervisor replied.

"I'm strong, Sir. I can help move those rocks much faster than your workers," said the strong man. "Let me show you."

He then carried two heavy stones at a time, and moved them with ease to the other end of the site. While he did this, Adam felt small; he couldn't even see his own shadow anymore because of

how big the strong man was. Conscious of his gigantic figure, the strong man looked at Adam and snickered. "We each have our natural role to play, and I guess this is not yours."

The supervisor was impressed with the speed at which the strong man could finish the work, so he hired him on the spot. Unfortunately, this meant that Adam was fired. He couldn't compete on strength nor speed. There was no argument to be made.

Recipe Book
Competition is about win-lose. It is focused on taking away your current and future opportunities.

Adam walked back home with a heavy heart, staring at nothing but the ground beneath his feet.

He had thought he had a job that would support his family for many months to come, or at least until he could find something better.

When he arrived home and shared the bad news, Tom didn't take it well.

"Now what are we going to do? How are we going to eat and pay the rent?! Things were much easier in SOMELAND! We had a secure future. Look at us now!" He began fretting at the sleeve of his shirt, biting his lip. "We were so much better off there."

Sara came in, closed the door behind her and took off her coat. "We are very far from SOMELAND, Tom! Why can't you accept that? Memories are like stones: they can either drown you or hold you up. Remember Father's story about the boy who lived in the past?"

Tom frowned at her and turned away, refusing to answer. Sara shook her head, disappointed. She and Tom had so rarely fought in SOMELAND, and yet now they seemed constantly at odds, and nothing she said appeared to get through to him. After a moment more of silence, Tom gave Sara an angry glance and walked out of the room, grumbling something under his breath.

Recipe Book

Sometimes people escape to the past to avoid the challenges of the present, thus sacrificing the present and the future.

Adam looked at Sara and asked, "Where have you been?"

"I've been exploring ANYLAND. A lot. I like it here, Adam." She smiled, more brightly than he'd expected in the circumstances.

Adam shook his head, too depressed to ask what she'd discovered or why she was so happy. He could only focus on figuring out a way to help support his family.

Mother would come by check up on them every now and then, trusting them to take care of each other while she cared for their father. It was difficult to persuade her, sometimes, that they were doing okay – she could feel the depression and irritation in the house – but Adam was determined that she didn't need to worry about them as well as Father. He made her visits as bright and cheerful as he could, though news about Father was rarely positive.

His condition did not seem to be improving, and there was a dark cloud looming over the family like never before. The nights when everyone would curl around the fire for entertainment and joy had been replaced by everyone huddling around just to keep warm. The fear was palpable. Tom seemed to be paralyzed with disappointment; he was clinging to the remnants of a reality that had passed away

As their situation got worse, Tom began trying their neighbors in the different apartments, the people who had failed to welcome them when they moved in, asking for some money for food. He had no luck, and he only grew angrier and more resentful every time they rejected him and shut the door in his face.

Recipe Book
Fear creates bondage.
You are only free when
you overcome your fears.

Adam kept on his search for a job. A few days later, he found one in a home for the elderly. He was in charge of sweeping the floors and keeping the place clean. He only received eight dollars a day, but for Adam, it was better than nothing.

One day, an elderly man saw Adam distressed while trying to fix the kitchen sink. The old man approached him with a warm smile on his face and said, "Need some help?"

He was a small man with glasses and white hair; he held a cane in order to stand up straight.

"I'm fine, Sir, thank you for the offer," Adam said quickly.

Then the old man did something that Adam would never have expected. He let go of the cane and struggled for a moment to find his balance, but then bent down and plucked the wrench from Adam's hand. It took him only 10 minutes to fix a problem that Adam had been struggling with for over an hour.

As the old man was getting up, he said, "You didn't expect that from an old man, did you? When you underestimate others, you only put limits on yourself.

Recipe Book

Never be quick to judge; surprises might be just a step away. Look beneath the surface.

As Adam left the elderly home that day, the old man's advice resonated. 'I only put limits on myself... but I'm merely a farmer without much education in a foreign land, so of course I have limited options,' Adam thought to himself.

When he got back home after a long day, Adam was disappointed to find that, yet again, Tom's entire day had been spent fiddling with the remote control, trying to figure out how to locate SOMELAND'S TV channel (STV).

"Why don't you try to find a job? There's a lot of construction going on in ANYLAND, and there are more opportunities here than in SOMELAND," said Adam.

"You want ME to carry rocks?" Tom said, rising from his seat and flushing with anger. "I won't carry rocks for a living! Do you understand? I'm a house designer, and a very, very good one! Are you seriously suggesting I should resort to manual labor? Do you remember who I used to be? I had a good job, stable, rewarding, respectable. Everybody looked up to me. I existed. I was SOMEBODY. Do you get what that means?" His voice cracked.

Adam sighed, trying to be patient. "Alright.

How about going to university to continue your studies so you can work as a builder again? As you said, you have a talent for building."

"You've got to be kidding me! I'm not going back to become a student again. I'm better than that. I don't need to study; I know everything there IS to know about building designs. It's this city that knows nothing about building, nothing at all.

Besides, I don't know the language well enough. and where are we going to get the money to pay for university?"

Sara, fed up with her brothers' continuous arguing, stood up. "Tom, it's not easy to start again... and from scratch. We all know that. But we have to try something! I have a project that I –"

Adam frowned. "But we're not starting from scratch, Sara. We already know a lot of things, and we have many resources that we can find and use. Staying at home and dreaming about going back to the past won't help! We have to get out there and do something, start taking action!"

Recipe Book

Arrogance prevents adaptation. Attitude and action that do not promote survival, lead to extinction. Arrogance can kill you.

Learning requires humility.

Recipe Book

Adaptation is not easy. It requires courage, flexibility, experimentation, risk taking, and hope in a brighter future.

One day, on his way back home, Adam was walking up the steps to the apartment and almost tripped over a small kite on the floor. He looked down and smiled. 'It must belong to the neighbor's boy, he thought. He picked up the kite and knocked on the neighbors' door. The boy's mother answered.

"Hello," Adam said. "I think this belongs to your son."

"Oh yes, he has been looking all over for it. Thank you so much!" replied the mother.

The boy suddenly appeared at the doorstep, jumping up and down with a large smile on his face, "Yay! You found it! You found it!" He looked up at Adam and said, "Wanna learn how to fly?" with a big grin.

Adam, so tired from his long day, let out a yawn and said; "I'm sorry, not today. Maybe another time."

The boy's smile faded and he replied quietly, "Okay, maybe another time then."

The days passed, with Adam working every day from sunrise to sunset to buy food with his small daily wage. One afternoon, a woman entered the elderly home where Adam worked. Her clothes were old and tattered.

"Are you looking for workers, Sir?"

she asked. "I'm looking for work, any kind of work, and I won't cost you much. In fact, I'll save you money because I'll work for less," she stated.

The woman offered to work for six dollars a day. She got the job, and Adam was asked to leave. Adam could not accept work for six dollars a day because the money was not enough to feed the family.

Adam went back home, dreading the expected discouraging comments from his brother.

And that's exactly what he got.

Recipe Book

Competition is a never-ending battle. Only your uniqueness will shield you from it.

"I told you there was no future for us in ANYLAND! I don't know why you even try."

"And I don't know why you don't! We're all in the same boat, Tom. You're the eldest and you're not rowing."

He wanted to say more, but Tom interrupted by slamming his hand on the table. "Listen, I'm not going back to being a student at this age. I won't sit in a class next to people half my age as if I'm starting all over again! I was a successful builder, respected by people and I was earning enough money to make a decent living. Now, look at me!"

Adam, boiling with anger, stood up. "ENOUGH ALREADY!"

It was the first time that Adam had ever raised his voice to his brother. Adam rarely let his anger get the better of him. He generally deferred to Tom's knowledge and experience, but the excruciating burden of family responsibility, and his frustration at his brother's implacable temperament outweighed his reserve. They needed to do something to keep their family together, and Tom's refusal was maddening.

"You are a talented person and you're wasting your life staying angry and bitter! It's time to

move past your complaints. What you went through, what we are all going through, is hard for all of us, not just you. But do you think if you stay down and angry, the solution will magically fall from the sky? NO! We need to keep moving forward even when circumstances make our life shift. You're not the only one who had to leave his home!" Adam turned and stormed out, slamming the door behind him.

Recipe Book
Sacrifices should be made wisely and only when necessary.

Adam had hopelessly tried to help his brother accept that their reality had changed and that there was no point in being stuck either in the good or in the bad memories of the past. He felt drained and his efforts wasted, and he was beginning to doubt whether he could influence Tom's attitude. At this point, he realized the only person that could change Tom was Tom, and Adam needed to keep focusing on encouraging himself and helping the family.

After hearing his brother's outburst, Tom sat alone for a long time. He was shocked that Adam had yelled at him. Although a small part of him agreed that Adam was right, he couldn't ignore the other part, which wanted something more from life, not just to make it through the day. He wanted something bigger. Unfortunately, he was not striving for what he wanted, because he was too caught up in the longing for the life he used to have.

Recipe Book

Conflict is a scary sacrifice of peace. If it is necessary do not avoid it, but be selective, be prepared, and be strong.

If you can't change a reality, either leave or adapt to make the best of it.

The next morning, the family woke up with nothing to eat. Adam, with a growling stomach, went to look for a job again. Tom went to the neighbors across the street to ask for money, hoping he would have better luck with neighbors in a different apartment complex. Again, however, he was met with slamming doors and irritation, and he returned home sour and empty-handed.

Adam wandered the streets, feeling lost, not sure what he was looking for. He was so angry with Tom, and he felt like he had no time or energy to try and understand Sara's perspective on their situation. On top of that, and something he tried to avoid thinking about, was his worry for his parents, particularly his father. Everything seemed to be getting harder, and the pressure was really starting to make him falter.

As he walked along with his hands in his pockets, he felt the pouch that Hank had once given him. He remembered the farming days with his mentor and all the wonderful memories from home came rushing back, making him feel nostalgic. He wished life could be like a chickpea again... simple, plentiful, and delicious.

Still thinking of the past, he looked up at the building in front of him, which was a small, plain-looking restaurant. He walked inside, and went to find the manager, trying to summon some hope. "Excuse me, Sir, are there any job openings?"

"You wanna work here, you start at the bottom washing dishes," replied the manager.

"I'll take it!" said Adam, who was so hungry for work that he didn't mind being at the bottom. He had never considered moving up based on merit. He would work harder than he had ever worked before.

He finished work late, but once the last counter had been wiped down and the final dish had been put away, he walked to the hospital, despite how tired he felt. He thought he ought to go and see his parents, and though he tried not to get his hopes too high, as the nurse walked him to his father's room, he couldn't help praying he might see some improvement.

The room was white and alien, and he felt a flash of relief that Mother stayed here with Father, rather than letting him face such a cold, clinical space alone. Father was asleep on the bed, and Mother sat in a chair, a book in her hands, dozing. She looked exhausted, and Adam made up his mind immediately that he would make no mention of their difficulties.

He sat in a nearby chair, and the movement woke her; she blinked, shifting, and almost dropping her book.

"Adam? Isn't it late?"

"Quite. I won't stay long, but I just wanted to see how you were."

She nodded, silent for a few seconds. "No change here, I'm afraid."

Adam tried not to let disappointment show in his face. "No better?"

"But no worse, either." She spoke firmly. "And you three?"

"We're doing fine. I got a new job today, working in a restaurant, plenty of opportunities to move up." He made his voice cheerful.

"And Sara and Tom?"

Adam hesitated, conviction wavering. "They're doing okay. Adjusting takes time."

She looked at him, then at the bed, obviously aware that he was withholding information for her sake. "I wish I could be at home with you."

"Father needs you more than we do right now.

Help him get well, and we'll be a family again." Adam leaned over to squeeze her hand, closing his eyes the better to picture that distant future.

Meanwhile, Tom was reflecting on his last conversation with Adam. He decided to use the Internet, something he was not familiar with, and try to look for a job.

While he was getting settled at the computer and trying to remember how to use it, Sara came in, closing the door behind her. She was tired of seeing Tom in a depressed, self-pitying and passive state, so she looked at him and said, "I want to show you something."

Tom had not been paying much attention to Sara's whereabouts, being too preoccupied with his own problems. But when he saw her with a big smile on her face, he couldn't help but feel curious, and perhaps even slightly more positive. If his sister was thrilled by something, it had to be a good thing. She grabbed his arm and pulled him up. "Come on, come on, it's really important!"

Tom had no choice but to follow Sara down to the basement of the building. They walked through a tiny corridor that seemed almost never-ending. Finally, as they came to the last door and she reached for the handle, Sara seemed to light up from within, beaming, her eyes shining with excitement. She tugged at his arm again, unable to help it.

"Inside," she said, "is the project I've been working on."

Recipe Book
Without the first step there is no journey to anywhere. Decide and act.

She opened the door, and inside the room, paintings were hung on every inch of the walls. Paintings of SOMELAND, portraits of their family, memories that they had, and paintings of a future she imagined having in ANYLAND. They were beautiful and inspiring, lit up with the color of young enthusiasm, keen joy, and – perhaps most importantly – hope.

Tom couldn't help but tear up. He was feeling so many things all at once. He was happy that his sister found a place for herself in ANYLAND by doing what she loved to do. At the same time, the paintings gave him a sense of her hope, which was almost like having some for himself. Through her eyes, he saw a visualization of how beautiful their life could be in ANYLAND, and a reminder of what it was like to be truly happy. In many of the pictures, Father was healthy and the family was together again. And wasn't that what this shift had been all about? Father getting healthy? For the first time in a year, Tom managed a real smile.

"How did... Where did... Wow, this is amazing," Tom exclaimed. "Why didn't you tell me about this before? I thought you told me everything..."

Sara scrubbed at her eyes, trying to blink back tears. Tom was her best friend, not just her

brother. "I tried many times, but every time I tried, you wouldn't even acknowledge me, you were too stuck in your own problems. I miss you, Tom... I want my brother back!"

With wet eyes, Tom hugged his sister. "I miss us too... Forgive me," he whispered, all choked up.

The emotions kept them silent for a few minutes. Tom took a few deep breaths, trying to get himself under control. He hadn't realized how bad things had become until now. He had been so consumed in his own disappointments that he had failed to see the positive things around him.

Recipe Book
Hope and abundance are everywhere. Self-pity is a destructive feeling.

"I'm really proud of you, Sara. How did you start doing all this?" he asked.

"My new art teacher has been working with me after she saw one of my paintings... helped me get all these supplies, encouraged me to keep discovering who I was as an artist," Sara said, pointing at her paintings. "When we first came to ANYLAND, I was like you. I wanted to go back to the familiar, to go back to life as we knew it, but then I discovered something greater than my worries and fears. It was magic!" "And I'm going to try to sell these at the next bazaar, so maybe I can help out with some of the bills," she said, raising her shoulders and looking up at him hopefully.

Later that night, the energy in the house seemed to have shifted positively. As Adam walked in, he was surprised and amused by how happy Sara seemed to be. She kept sharing jokes with Tom, and Tom was actually laughing. Something was different, and Adam could not help but smile.

Sara could not contain her joy as she showed Adam what she had done.

Recipe Book
Living purposefully makes you shine.

The people that you surround yourself with will shape your life. Embrace the positive and protect yourself from negativity, even if it comes from those closest to you.

Life went on as steadily as it could for the following months. Unfortunately, Adam was still carrying most of the weight. He kept working long hours with no days off, but he got to work in the kitchen of a restaurant. He was eager to observe the chef and his team preparing delicious meals. Soon he was promoted to food prep. He only made fifty more cents an hour and mostly chopped onions, but he was happy to be moving forward.

Tom and Sara tried helping as much as they could by selling some of her paintings. It took a while, but eventually, Sara was able to sell a few of them, and to help Adam pay the rent and medical bills. She was surprised to find that she was not sad to sell them, but rather happy. She could picture them hanging in someone's living room or above their bed, think of people appreciating them, and feeling brighter about the world.

With Sara finding her gift of art, Tom saw a glimmer of hope and decided that it was time for him to try and stop clinging to the past and accept his new reality. He even started to search for universities that he could attend to follow his dream of becoming a builder.

But things are never stable for too long...

One day, while Adam was washing dishes, he overheard a conversation between the restaurant manager and a man with his son.

"But I already have someone washing the dishes," said the manager.

"I understand," said the man. "Just consider this. I have many years of work experience in restaurants. My son has a beautiful voice that your customers will find really entertaining. I'm prepared to work with my son for less than 10 dollars a day! We can prep your food, wash your dishes, and provide a show you could sell tickets for. Just think about the extra value you'll be getting!"

There was silence for a few seconds. Adam's heart was pounding as he anticipated the bad news.

It came. The manager felt terrible, but his food costs had been out of control lately, and he needed any extra money he could get.

Adam, yet again, was asked to leave.

Recipe Book

Don't compete. Create your own game.

With a combination of shock, fatigue, and concerns about the future, Adam walked home, trying to process what had just happened.

Tom was working on the computer, looking at universities, when Adam walked in the door, completely defeated. There was no need for either of them to say anything. Their faces said it all. Adam and Tom sat down silently, staring at an empty wall, feeling devastated.

Without Adam's income, the bills started to pile up once again.

"The landlord sent us a final warning. We will be evicted from here if we don't pay by the end of the month," said Tom, as he paced back and forth. "I thought for a while that staying here and trying might actually work, but look at us! We'd better off returning home. I went to the hospital yesterday, partly to reassure them we're okay. Dad seems to be slowly recovering. Maybe we can continue the treatment back there. Mother's been by his side the whole time, so surely she must know what to do by now..."

Tom knew, even as he spoke, that it was the technology and medicine that was healing his father. That same kind of medical care did not exist anywhere else in the world.

With a broken spirit and a tightening feeling in his stomach, Tom added, "I tried some of our neighbors again, since it's been a while, and I thought maybe they'd take pity on us, especially since you returned their kite. They wouldn't even open the door for me, at least until they got fed up with my knocking.

"The angry neighbor asked if I had any shame. They said times are hard all around and they can barely take care of themselves. So much for this being a land of opportunity."

Adam patted Tom on the knee. He understood where his brother was coming from now.

"I have never felt so humiliated in my life," said Tom with teary eyes, remembering the days of his past success and the money and respect that he had once had.

Tom was mostly ruled by his fear. He had had a good life before, and he was scared, scared to start anew, so at any sign of trouble, he retreated back to his comfort zone: the past.

Recipe Book

Every time you over-glorify the past as having been better, you're worsening a future that hasn't even had a chance to exist yet.

Adam, angry at strangers for making his brother so upset, went over to the neighbor's and knocked hard on the door. The little boy answered with a smile on his face, and, suddenly full of excitement, grabbed Adam by the arm and dragged him inside.

Startled by the behavior of the boy, Adam followed.

"Do you want to fly today?" asked the little boy.

Not knowing what else to say, and not wanting to disappoint the little boy yet again, Adam agreed. "Umm... sure, why not?"

The boy led Adam to an open window, where a kite was flying in the sky, the strings rigged expertly around various items of furniture. The boy handed the strings to Adam.

"You let out the string so the kite can fly, but then you have to tighten the string so the kite doesn't lose balance and fall."

Adam felt wobbly and not confident when trying to let the kite soar. It kept falling over and over again, but he didn't feel inclined to give in. He began to work out how to tug the strings, how to loosen them, and the kite responded, dipping and twirling satisfyingly in the breeze.

"It's okay, you almost have it. My mom always tells me to keep trying," said the boy, still grinning.

Adam smiled back at him. "Does she? My mom says that too."

Adam thanked the boy and went home. He felt like he had done more than just fly a kite. He felt like he had realized that Tom had been a burden on him, and that the little boy had taught him how to fly free from that weight, and the importance of not giving up on himself. Tom wasn't a stone he was paid to carry from one side of a job site to the other. Tom wasn't his job. Adam deserved to be happy.

Adam looked at his brother with mixed feelings of compassion and frustration. Many questions raced through his head about Tom: Why are you doing this to yourself and to people around you? Why are you so focused on your past wounds, not believing in your worth, in your ability to re-create yourself? Why are you selling yourself short, imprisoned by the fear of a fresh start?

Then he realized that, in many ways, he was doing the same, so how could he blame Tom?

"I need to go for a walk, to clear my head," said Adam.

Recipe Book

You need to take care of yourself first so that you can take care of others.

Without a clear purpose, choices become re-active, resilience declines and life becomes harder.

Walking slowly at dusk, with his hands in his pockets and his head down, Adam thought. I've accepted that I can't go back to SOMELAND, so why should I keep settling for any job that comes along?

He walked for hours without even knowing where he was going, until he came across the town square. Kids were flying kites in the air, carefree and curious.

Flying the kite had made him feel like a child again – happy, wild, and free, open to any possibility that might come. As he watched the bobbing kites, something else caught his eye.

A street performer had come into the square, and was standing in the center, setting up for a show. Within minutes of him starting to juggle, people were gathering. Then more people came. Then even more, until the performer was fully surrounded and barely visible. Everyone was enjoying the show, especially the performer as he interacted with the audience and accepted their gifts of spare change.

The street performer amused Adam; his obvious enthusiasm was contagious. Adam decided to talk to him at the end of his act. When the crowd had cleared, he put his hands in his pockets, took a deep breath, and approached.

"Sir, where did you learn how to perform like that?" Adam asked.

"I taught myself mostly... only finished elementary schooling," said the performer.

"Oh, wow. Really?" Adam asked.

"Yes, I've always loved to perform, so I kept at it every day. You know what they say about practice makes perfect. I'm certainly not perfect yet, but I do practice. I even used to practice in front of the mirror at home for hours because it made me so darn happy."

"I can certainly see it makes you happy." Adam nodded.

"I couldn't afford to perform in a theater, so I had to play the hand I was dealt. I learned to make the streets my stage, and this way I can share my talent with others and learn from their comments. I like the freedom of street performance. It makes me easier to talk to, and I sure do love it when the audience talks to me, especially the kids."

Adam nodded, watching a grinning child approach, hand outstretched with spare change.

The performer smiled, then crouched down, produced a balloon, and – with a few deft twists – handed it over as an unmistakable blue giraffe.

"Wow. Balloon animals too? "

The performer laughed. "It's only for the children, but I can make you one if you'd like."

Adam smiled back.

"So how did you get to the point where you could make a living doing what you love?"

"Getting feedback improved my performance, and that made the crowd happier, rewarding me with more money and encouragement and... the cycle continues," said the performer.

Recipe Book
Always, always stay close to your customers.

"What do you mean?"

"It's like in relationships. The more love is given, the more love is received, or in my case money, respect, and more work," replied the performer.

"So, you are doing this for the money?"

"No, I don't do this for the money," said the performer, shaking his head. "If I wanted to make money, there are plenty of quicker ways to do so and maybe even to get rich. I'm just happy doing what I love and sharing it with others... I see money as a way that people reward me for making them happy. When you give from your heart, the reward is more generous... It's simple really."

"Are you saying money is not important?" Adam frowned, thinking of the bills piling up, the empty cupboards, and the hospital treatments they had to afford.

"I didn't say that." The performer shook his head again. "When one is focused on enjoying his unique gifts and sharing them with others, rewards, including money, will eventually follow as a result. Think of the world's top performers or athletes... Would they have become famous or rich if they did not work hard to perfect their talent and share it with the world?"

Recipe Book

Purpose does not have to sustain you financially. At the same time it does not have to be charitable.

"Do you have big dreams?" asked Adam.

"I hope to be the best that I can be, and make my performances touch as many lives as possible. It's not just about dreaming big, it's about finding and being me. That's what really matters."

"So that's it?" Adam raised his eyebrows in total amazement, but he still wasn't fully convinced. "Isn't it embarrassing to perform on the street like this?"

"Sir, if you want my genuine opinion, true embarrassment is when one does not have something valuable to offer others or to add beauty to the world. I'm not forcing people to watch me. I'm simply doing what I love to do."

"And don't you worry about competition?" Adam couldn't see how the performer could keep street crowds to himself.

"I don't think about what other people do unless I want to learn from them. Every person is gifted in a special way and people get to choose the way they express their talents. Besides, there are enough people to appreciate every kind of talent," he added with a wink. "Frankly, I would love to meet someone who can do what I do: we could collaborate. It hasn't happened yet."

Recipe Book

Uniqueness neutralizes competition. Innovation maintains your uniqueness.

"Is this your 'Recipe' for success?" asked Adam.

The performer laughed. "It's up to you if you wish to call it success. I don't think about success as winning or being the best. Those are just terms that people use to feel that they are better than others. All I know is that I feel I was born to perform and entertain others, to bring moments of joy to their lives and to mine. Performing is my purpose; it gives my life special meaning. Performing comes naturally to me... It is ME, and because I enjoy it so much, I find it almost effortless because it's the most authentic expression of myself."

Adam drifted off in contemplation for a few moments, allowing the exchange to sink in and his brain to process what the man had said. Finally, he looked up and spoke again.

"Sorry for keeping you, but I just have one more question. I heard that there are new rules to ban street performers. Is that true?"

"I don't know for sure," replied the performer.

"If it's true, will you stop performing?"

"I am sorry, but I didn't catch your name, Sir."

"Oh, how rude of me. My name is Adam."

"What do you do for a living, Adam?" The

performer looked at him keenly, head tilted to one side.

"Oh, you know. Odd jobs," said Adam, feeling self-conscious, "We all have bills to pay."

The performer pondered for a few seconds.

"In the end, we all have to do what has to be done to survive. But I don't think that means we need to settle. I think there's always an abundance of opportunities, creativity, and resources to allow us to stay true to ourselves. The way I see it, our life isn't just about surviving, or losing our true selves to fit changing situations… that would be a kind of dying from the inside. Let me ask you this: what was the last job you had that you enjoyed?"

Adam felt around in his pocket, his hand closing over the precious packet there.

"Chickpeas… I used to farm them and then when times got tight, I found creative ways to make various dishes with…" Adam laughed at the simplicity of it. "Chickpeas."

"There you have it. We are blessed with lots of options and even if it doesn't seem that way, we can always get creative. It's not like I have to rely on one type of food to survive, just give me a few ingredients and I can create a bunch of dishes, you know what I mean?" The performer smiled.

Adam grinned, the wheels already churning in his head.

"So, in my case, if I couldn't perform in public squares, I wouldn't start working in real estate or other jobs. I might start performing in cafes, restaurants, or teaching, or I could even move to another city. My purpose does not limit me. This isn't simple, but it does make taking risks a lot easier," said the performer. "I'm sorry about rambling on, but your questions are deep, and I could talk about this all day!"

Recipe Book
Purpose can manifest itself in many forms.

"You have no idea how important this conversation is to me, when everything around me is changing," said Adam. "The truth is I'm not from around here. I come from a faraway land that you probably haven't heard of and my story is... well..." Adam paused, and decided he didn't feel like launching into it. "Going back to your point, it seems that lately, I've been so focused on just fighting for whatever job I can get that I forgot about what I truly love and what I'm good at."

The performer thought for a few seconds and then signaled Adam to follow him.

"It's easy to get caught in this trap," he said. "Take this playground for example..." As he started to walk, he pointed at two children arguing in the sandbox.

"It's my shovel!" said the little girl, clinging tightly to one side of it.

"No, I saw it first!" said the other one, pulling it towards her.

"Look how they are fighting over one shovel when there are a bunch of other ones lying around," said the performer.

"For some reason, we believe that things will

eventually run out; that we either fight or lose," he added. "It's a huge playground and yet they're fighting over one shovel. Plus, the sandbox doesn't go anywhere but to a wooden bottom, a dead end. Imagine if they both grabbed a shovel and dug outside of the box. Who knows what they might find?"

Adam nodded, thoughtful, listening to the sound of children shrieking and playing.

"Look around us, Adam. What do you see?"

Caught off guard, Adam looked at the performer, confused.

The performer then continued, "We each are so different and have something beautiful to offer the world. We just have to be aware of it, live it, enjoy it and share it."

"Wow... Where did you learn all this?" asked Adam, with his eyes wide open, feeling awed. "Sorry for looking surprised, but frankly I didn't expect a street performer to talk with such depth."

"I grew up in a small town. Things were slower there, which gave me a lot of time to think. After all, the first person I ever had to learn how to entertain was myself."

"Where are you from?" Adam asked.

"Oh... I came here a long time ago from a far-away place called SOMELAND," the performer said. "Perhaps I'll see you again sometime, Adam." He waved and turned to walk away.

Recipe Book

Humans are designed to seek beyond basic survival. We are made for fulfillment.

Abundance and creativity make it possible to stay true to your special purpose, even when the surrounding environment changes.

Adam stared after him, frozen, ideas and questions pouring through his mind.

He began wandering the streets of the city, turning the man's words over and over in his mind as he walked. The rhythm of his feet on the pavement accompanied his thoughts, and he walked for hours, reflecting on what had happened. The simple philosophies which had been laid out to him brought so many different questions and perspectives.

"Why has my thinking been small and petty?

Why do I think of myself as not being good enough?

Why did I waste all this time instead of appreciating it?

What is to become of the rest of my life? Will I carry rocks or sweep floors? Beg for jobs that will barely feed my family?

If I die soon, what was the point of my life?

Why did I not see the world's abundance and opportunities?

How much of the world's beauty did I experience?

What would people say about the life I've lived?"

He couldn't hold back his tears as the questions flooded in, and they kept coming, even as he walked on, until he found himself in front of the restaurant he had been fired from the day before. Totally drained, he sat under a tree facing the restaurant and slept.

Recipe Book

We are designed to seek meaning. Without meaning the heart will know neither peace nor joy.

"Wake up! Wake up! Go away," shouted a man, shaking Adam's shoulder hard. "Beggars aren't allowed to sleep in front of my shop. You will scare away the customers!"

Adam woke up, stunned and humiliated.

He slowly got up as the shop owner kept glaring and pushing him to leave. As he stood up, he noticed that something had fallen out of his pocket. It was the pouch that Hank had given him. Inside it were six dried chickpeas. He took out the chickpeas, looked at them for a while, and then it hit him...

'Stay true to yourself.' Hank's words echoed in his thoughts. He wondered how he had let himself drift so far away. He couldn't even recognize himself anymore.

Suddenly, everything made sense.

It was a beautiful day, with a clear sky, a fresh breeze, and brilliant sunlight. With his eyes fixed on the restaurant and with his mind recollecting the events of yesterday, Adam felt inspired to his core. He pulled out his old notebook, which he still carried for the sake of comfort, and started to write.

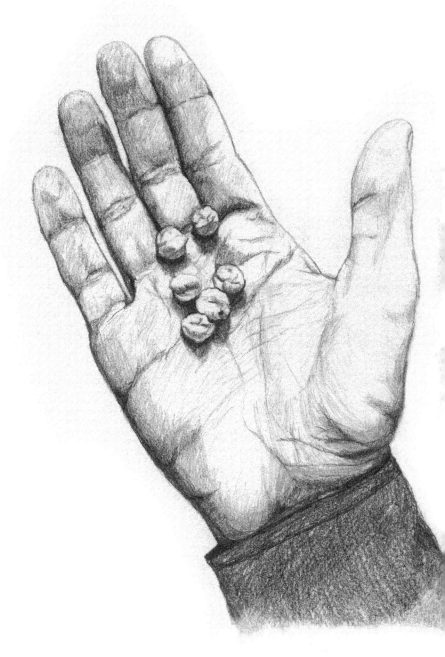

It had been ages since he had last flipped through it, and it felt good to put his thoughts on paper, though his hand could hardly keep up with everything he wanted to say.

He asked himself:

"What am I really good at doing?

What uniqueness can I share with others like the street performer was sharing?

What can I do to live according to my true self, rather than just being like everyone else?

Am I doing what I truly want to do?

What is it that I can do that adds value to people so that I deserve their rewards?

What would I do if I were not chained by fears or responsibilities?

What opportunities would I lose if I didn't dream beyond fulfilling my duties?"

As he reflected further, Adam found himself walking towards the restaurant where he used to work. At the back of the restaurant was a tiny garden, just a scrap of earth, but a few fresh vegetables and herbs were bedded down in the soil. Looking at them made him think of the farm at SOMELAND. The smell of thyme, mint, and

Recipe Book

Before you jump to the other side, make sure the greener grass there is not fake. Often our greatest growth opportunity is where we are now.

basil rose to his face on the fresh morning air.

It felt like the last piece of the puzzle to give him courage to do what he should've done a long time ago. He opened the restaurant door, took a deep breath, and stepped inside.

"I've noticed that half of the seats in the restaurant are usually empty and, based on the dishes I scraped, there seems to be a lot of food waste," he blurted as soon as he located the manager, without so much as a greeting first.

The manager's jaw dropped; he was dumbfounded.

"Excuse me... What are you saying?"

"I'm saying we need to find a way to fill the empty seats: we should have people standing in line to eat here. People should become obsessed with our food!"

"OUR Food?! Weren't you fired yesterday?!" The manager paused for a moment, astounded by the whole conversation. "And how do you suggest we do that?"

"I will make it happen. I know what I'm doing and how to go forward. I've got this!" said Adam, setting his shoulders squarely. His eyes shone with confidence as he glanced around the place, seeing everything which could be changed.

The owner gave Adam a long, cynical look.

"Hmmm... YOU will make it happen! And how will you do that, Mr. Best? We've been trying for years and that was even before these restaurants opened around us. What can YOU do that is so different?"

"I'll cook something special!"

"YOU... will cook?"   asked the manager, in disbelief. "You are a dishwasher or a busboy at best!"

"No. I'm not. I'm very talented in the kitchen and I know my food!" Adam replied, throwing his head back confidently. "Here's my proposition: let me try it out. If you like my cooking, you'll take me back to work as a chef in your kitchen, paid as you think fit." He looked the man straight in the eyes.

"I'll take full responsibility. You have nothing to lose." Adam was confident that the manager would like his cooking. Back in SOMELAND, he often cooked at home, and all his dishes were extremely popularwith his family, neighbors, and friends. He had always had a passion for cooking, but had never thought of pursuing it as a career.

Hummus, a paste made from the chickpeas of his farm, was one of his specialties, and Hank's favorite dish.

The story he had told himself all his life was 'I'm not good enough: there is nothing that I can offer that is significant and worthy of admiration. I am just an ordinary person. There is nothing special about me.' But all this time he had failed to see that his cooking lit up people's faces and left a warm feeling in their bellies, a feeling that went beyond just a satisfying meal.

Recipe Book
You become the stories you tell yourself. You are the author of your own story.

Adam returned home, nervous about telling his family what had happened. He was expecting his mother to visit that morning, but he was not expecting the sight which greeted him when he opened the door. His mother was standing by the window and, in a chair near the fire, sat his father, Sara on his lap, Tom at his side.

Adam rushed to hug them both. "Is everything okay? What are you doing home?"

"Healing," his father said, reaching to put his arms around Adam's neck for a hug. "At home from now on, at the home you all made for us."

Adam looked in his eyes and knew that his father was going to make it. He knew that his sacrifice had paid off. That made his big news about the restaurant seem less relevant, but somehow even sweeter.

He wasn't sure what reaction to expect, and was slightly hesitant to tell them the news, but when he looked around at them and thought of everything their family had been through, his anxiety was no match for his growing confidence.

"You as a chef?!" a startled Tom said. "You always did make the best hummus!"

Adam, placing his hand on his heart, smiled,

and said, "I love cooking... It's weird that it hadn't hit me until now."

Adam was truly relieved by his brother's reaction. For once, it seemed like Tom could see some potential for at least one of them in ANYLAND. It was though he had found a way to visualize the possibility of a brilliant future, if only for Adam, instead of feeling that they had to give up their dreams, their happiness, and a chance to make a difference in life.

Tom had stopped believing in himself and kept running away from any major challenge. At least for now, with Adam's new hope, he might see a way past these fears and perhaps one day make his way to a future of his own.

"I'm so proud of you, son," said Adam's mother, with a warm smile on her face.

"Me too," said his father, squeezing his shoulder. He was finally getting better, and seeing his children happy made the recovery process faster.

Sara did not say anything; she just threw her arms around Adam's neck and closed her eyes, squeezing her brother tightly.

Recipe Book

Whatever hardship you face, someone has overcome something harder.

You can handle any situation in your life. Despair, blame and self-pity are useless.

Adam had never felt as good as he did strutting into the restaurant. It was as if a mountain had been lifted from his shoulders. Suddenly, it wasn't about his painful past, his present insecurities, or his worries about the future. Now was about one thing only: fulfilling his passion for cooking food that people would love.

His confidence was growing and he walked more firmly, taller, faster. Even his tone changed when he greeted people at the restaurant very early in the morning. He was radiating happiness and people felt it.

The manager of the restaurant stood in amazement as he observed Adam. He looked at him over the top of his glasses as Adam handled kitchen appliances and cooking ingredients with ease, experience, and elegance. It was as if he had been a professional cook for years: everything was flowing effortlessly.

Anticipation rose by the minute. As the food was being prepared, the manager seemed more anxious than Adam.

"Enjoy your meal." Adam bowed the manager towards the table, beautifully set, with a mouth-watering dish waiting.

The manager then took a bite... A couple of seconds passed by, and Adam remained calm. The kitchen crew, however, stood there, biting their lips, waiting in anticipation.

As the manager took another bite, his face remained blank. He chewed slowly, and then looked at Adam with a furrowed brow. Then, after a moment more, he smiled. "Now that's something," he said.

A week later, the menu of the restaurant was re-vamped with all of Adam's new dishes. The number of customers quickly increased, and waiting lists became a standard, first at weekends, then every night.

People, quite simply, loved Adam's cooking, especially the hummus. This exquisite dish was seasoned with herbs and spices similar to the ones he used to collect on the farm in SOMELAND. "More hummus" became a standard customer request.

Recipe Book

To build sustainable success, create raving customers who voluntarily promote the value of your purpose.

A couple of years later, after one of the busiest days the restaurant had ever had, the manager pulled Adam aside and said, "Let's walk and talk."

"I feel that it's only fair that you get part of the business that you have miraculously created over the past two years." The manager had quickly become dependent on the popularity of Adam's cooking and wanted to keep him satisfied and secure.

Things were finally coming together. Adam had already paid the long overdue rent and started furnishing the family apartment. Debts were paid, and the kitchen was stacked with food for the first time in years.

Adam's parents felt healthier and looked younger as they saw life starting to smile back at their family. Adam was even able to lend Tom money for him to begin his studies.

Adam's life was falling into place, and he was finally happy...

But then... shift happened again!

The restaurant caught on fire and, once again, Adam's job vanished overnight. When he first looked at the burnt-out shell, he wondered if it would be like the other times, if he would find himself pacing the streets in a lost daze, but he didn't feel that way. He didn't feel lost at all. He felt like this was an opportunity, and he knew exactly where he was heading.

Recipe Book
The future is unpredictable, always be prepared for unexpected shifts.

A friend offered Adam a job as a real estate broker, with the promise of a substantial income that Adam wouldn't have dreamed of a month ago. But Adam declined without hesitation. He had discovered his purpose and was determined to hold on to it even if circumstances changed. It wasn't about securing ANY future anymore, but about the future that was a reflection of his authentic self. He had tasted the joy of doing what he felt he was born to do, and was determined not to let go at any price.

Many of Adam's loyal customers were wealthy and admired him a lot. They offered him opportunities. They kept requesting his services, so he started to cater for private events, and made deliveries upon request.

Eventually, an entrepreneur offered him a partnership at his restaurant, with full control over the menu. But this wasn't enough. Feeling confident, Adam decided to make it on his own and open a little restaurant called "A Taste of Purpose." Designed by Tom and decorated by Sara, the restaurant brought a lot of opportunities for all three of them.

"A Taste of Purpose" became the talk of the town, and people booked days in advance to secure a table.

Recipe Book

You were born to be your true self.

Stay true to your purpose and life will take care of you.

Soon there was another restaurant, then another... and the rented place where Adam lived became a distant memory as the family moved to a beautiful house Surrounded by gardens.

Adam's success didn't distance him from the kitchen. He began experimenting with new recipes and improving his craft. Those closest to him, specifically his mother, always lent a helping hand and kept him grounded. Although many restaurants and chefs tried to imitate him, none were able to copy his signature dishes.

Recipe Book
To always grow, always learn, always innovate.

"I am happy that ANYLAND as a country is becoming a culinary center," he once said in a TV interview, when asked about competition. "There's a place in this world for all 'tastes' of beauty."

Soon after, Adam established a cooking school. People came from different corners of the world to attend, and many of the graduates moved on to find their own cooking identity and became successful, some even globally renowned. He didn't only teach cooking, but the art of adding beauty to the world through distinguished culinary experiences.

Along the way, the progress of Adam's life continued inspiring both his siblings. Tom and Sara kept trying to find their own way. Sara became known for her art exhibitions. She was clear about her path from the start.

Tom, however, in spite of his remarkable talent for design, still had his ups and downs because a part of him remained in the past and could not fully adapt to the changes in his life. He never took advantage of the opportunities that the shifts in his life offered him.

The first thing he tried was taking a job as an employee in one of the largest construction companies in ANYLAND. It didn't even begin well; from the start, he felt he knew better, WAS better, than anyone around him. That included the supervisor. His attitude, his irritation, and his refusal to change his methods did nothing to help the team spirit, and demoralized those working around him. The employers let him go before he quit, but it wouldn't have continued for long regardless.

Despite this shift, other contractors offered him work, recognizing the talent in his designs and the skills he had – especially after he had designed and constructed his brother's increasingly famous restaurants. He was offered a chance to work with other talented constructors to form an elite company, but again, his partners found him impossible to work with. He refused to accept that design concepts which worked in SOMELAND didn't work for ANYLAND. He criticized any strategies unique to ANYLAND, undermined his colleagues, and created a tense, negative atmosphere which derailed their progress.

His fears, negativity, and ego remained barriers, blocking his path, and bringing difficulties to all aspects of his life. He married, but again carried expectations and remnants from SOMELAND, refusing to change, to face up to challenges, to recognize when he was wrong. His wife tried to help him, as Adam had tried, but he wouldn't listen to her.

In the end, the marriage couldn't be saved; his wife, worried that she would constantly be dragged down by him, decided to leave him and move on with her life.

Concerned about how Tom would deal with such a dramatic shift, Adam gave his brother the money for a solo venture, thinking perhaps he could make it alone if he couldn't work with others. However, Tom struggled to work with clients, struggled to let anyone make suggestions about their designs, or tell him what they wanted, and his company went bankrupt in the end. He considered, for some time, going back to SOMELAND, but he never made the leap. After all, it was wonderful in his memories, but he was afraid that in going back, he would find it was not the same. So he struggled on, unable to live in the present or work with others.

Recipe Book

Attitudes are contagious, make sure yours is worth catching. Positive attitudes inspire.

Although he was concerned for his brother, and sorry for his problems, Adam continued with his own life, helping Tom out whenever he saw an opportunity, and focusing on his own journey. He felt he had much to do in the world outside of his own family concerns, and needed to put his energy into it.

Perhaps the proudest moment of Adam's life was when he was honored for creating a foundation that helped feed people in poor countries and raised healthy food awareness among school children.

He was often featured in newspapers and magazines, and was a frequent guest on TV shows.

Just like a beautiful dream, Adam's life transformed the day he looked within and rediscovered his true self, accepted it with compassion, gratitude, and grace, celebrated it, and shared it with others.

The love, respect, and admiration that he received for enriching people with his gifts healed many of his past wounds. Negativity became petty and unworthy of his attention and time. **No matter what life threw at him he was ready to handle it because he knew who he was and where he was going.**

Recipe Book
Being extraordinary means...being more you!

Purpose is about service. Service attracts love. Love heals wounds and leads to joy.

Many years and an MBA from a well-known ANYLAND business school later, Adam gave a keynote speech at a prominent business university where his son was studying.

In an interview held after his speech, a student asked Adam, "From a business school perspective, isn't purpose romantic or spiritual... a La-La Land concept?"

Adam smiled and shook his head. "On the contrary, business has to add value to people to remain sustainable. This is what purpose is: your unique way of making other people's lives better. 'Uniqueness' keeps competition away, while sharing your gifts with others adds value and retains the loyalty of your customers."

He reflected for a few seconds. "It's because of clarity of purpose that we were able to build a successful enterprise. Purpose is the foundation of our strategy. It's the prime motivator for brilliant execution."

"Is purpose really that important? Does it make life easy?" asked the student.

"From my business experience, purpose gave me focus: it helped simplify my decisions and mobilize my team. It even made failing tolerable.

It opened my eyes to numerous possibilities. Our business success would not have happened if it weren't for our clear sense of purpose," Adam replied. "But don't get me wrong, we made a lot of mistakes along the way. Life is never easy, but with purpose, you have a compass to guide you."

Recipe Book
Purpose is life's compass.
It gives you direction.

"But can't the competition copy you and take away your advantage?"

"Think of it this way: nobody can be you. Nobody can be the exact same expression of you. Not now... not ever... Especially if you keep enriching your experiences and expanding on your authentic self. Of course, there are others who will try to be like you... But even if they succeeded, they would be merely an imitation," Adam said, smiling and shaking his head.

"Are you ever scared that your luck may change?"

"No, because I don't rely on luck. It's too risky, too unstable," replied Adam. "Just like I've learned not to rely on my circumstances. Circumstances are always changing. I've had to adapt and evolve my ways of sharing my best with the world. My focus is on creating value that reflects my uniqueness, regardless of the shifts in life... In fact, I've made change and uncertainty my friends, because they keep giving me new ways of living my purpose."

"Is having a clear purpose enough?" The student glanced up from scribbling in his notebook, and looked at Adam.

Recipe Book

**Change and uncertainty
are just natural processes:
make them your friends.**

**Voluntary change
should only be initiated
when it is necessary or
purposeful.**

"Developing a clear purpose is just the beginning. You still have to design a fitting strategy and ensure a good execution. You can think of the relationship between purpose, strategy, and execution as flowers in a vase. Purpose is the vase that is fixed, strategy is the choice of flowers and execution is the way the flowers are arranged. You can have several arrangements of flowers to fit the changing seasons, but the vase remains the constant. Strategy should be designed and executed within the frame of purpose," Adam said. "The three of them together add beauty."

Recipe Book
You need strategy and execution to transform your purpose into action.

"Is purpose like finding your passion?" asked the student.

"Passion is about intense emotions that can be blinding and dangerous if not directed properly." Adam pushed his hair back and looked at the student before continuing.

"Purpose is different. Purpose is about sharing your best with the world so that it becomes a better place for all. It's about promoting well-being. Purpose is about channeling the energy of passion like a laser beam in a direction that is good for you and for others."

Stimulated by the insights, the student looked at Adam, eyes hopeful. "Would it be possible to schedule another interview for our magazine's special edition on Purpose?"

"By all means," said Adam, "but not before next month. We are busy now preparing for a worldwide launch of our new business concept. In the meantime, there are a few insights and questions that I would like you to think about." Adam handed the student a copy of his recipe book, which summarized the lessons life had taught him over the years.

Recipe Book

Purpose and passion are not the same. Passion is immense energy. Purpose is about using this energy to make life better for yourself and others.

"Thank you," said the student, "I look forward to reading this and answering the questions. Out of curiosity though, may I ask what the concept of your new business is?"

With a smile, Adam said. "We will be revealing it soon through the media."

"By the way," said the student, "you haven't told me yet how a person or an organization can find their purpose."

"Unfortunately, we have not been trained to think in terms of purpose as individuals or organizations. It's never easy. Discovering your personal or organizational purpose is a process that needs patience, reflection, and experimentation. It's the most important duty towards yourself and your company," replied Adam. "But I will give you a tip that is actually one of my favorite clichés... As a person, start by looking within your heart."

Recipe Book

You owe it to yourself to look within and find your purpose.

The biggest tragedy of your life is being aware of your purpose and not living it.

"Would you say a little more?"

"You are a good interviewer," Adam replied with a smile. "**Ask yourself questions like: When do I shine? What makes my heart dance? What activities make me lose track of time? When do I get special praise from people? Whom do I want to help and how? What am I ready to do even for free because of the joy it gives me and the value it creates for others? How would I spend my life if I had no insecurities? What would I do if success was guaranteed and failing was impossible? What would my life be about if I had no fears?**"

"These are deep questions," said the student.

"They sure are," said Adam. "That is because purpose lives in our core. To find it, we have to dig deep."

"What about organizations?" asked the student.

"I have observed that most organizations, unfortunately, still don't think seriously in terms of purpose because they consider it a fluffy concept that has a sort of 'Zen' feel." Adam frowned and shook his head, adjusting one of his sleeves "That is true," replied the student. "When asked, most of the CEOs who come to speak at our business school say the purpose of their organizations is to make money."

"I bet you, though, if this question was asked to the founders of these organizations, you would have received a different answer," said Adam.

"Of course companies want to make money, but if one investigates how companies started and what kept them in business, it would become evident that the founders had clear ideas in mind on how to offer unique value to the people whom they wanted to serve. Most enduring organizations started with purposeful ideas that attracted money, not vice versa."

"I see what you mean," said the student. "In fact, when entrepreneurs talk about their stories they often talk fervently about the "ideas" and not just the "money" that got them to create the organizations they founded." He paused for a moment, looking thoughtful. "So how can organizations think about their purpose?"

"Well... I believe there are a number of questions to ask: **Firstly, what was the purpose of the original idea behind the creation of our organization? Why did clients buy our products** or services, and why do they continue to buy them? Why do they choose us and not others? What is special about what we do that keeps clients coming back? What is the core value that we add to the lives of our customers? What do clients tell other people when they refer them to us? How do clients perceive us compared to other organizations in the same industry? What difference do we want to make in the lives of the people whom we serve and in what special way do we express who we are?"

"I can see how these are fundamental questions," said the student.

"Exactly so," Adam replied. "Purpose-led thinking should shape the culture of any organization that wants to stay in business... I like to call it PURPOSESHIP.

My advice to you as business students is that, if you want to have successful, abundant and fulfilling lives, build and lead organizations where the words purpose and adaptability are carved in the hearts, minds, and actions of each of your employees... the rest is detail."

"May I trouble you with a final question?" asked the student. "What did life teach you?"

Adam took a few moments to silently reflect on his long and difficult journey.

"Life taught me that we are wired to seek well-being, that there is a wisdom to life that we should trust, follow, and learn from. That life for us can't simply be about surviving, but about the

Recipe Book
The key to survival and growth is clarity of purpose and adaptability to change.

real joy that comes from the growth that leads to fulfillment.

Every person by default is designed to become the best version of themselves and is capable of doing so. This is achieved by discovering and embracing one's uniqueness and sharing it with others. To sum it up: I would say my motto in life is quite simple: ENJOY, SHARE, and GROW all the beauty that we are."

The student was silent for a moment, thinking over everything which had been said. "I feel lucky that I am learning about purpose this early on. I think many miss out on this way of thinking and waste their lives without finding their uniqueness and living it."

"Yes, it would be wonderful to develop a clear purpose at a young age," replied Adam. "However, it is NEVER too late. Some of the people didn't discover their uniqueness until much later, and it never stopped them from making a good impact on life".

"Did you expect to be so successful?" asked the student.

"I was confident that our food would be appreciated and that our first restaurant would keep us busy, but frankly, not in my wildest dreams did I imagine that we would grow so much. The expansion wasn't really planned, but I guess when people discover and enjoy your uniqueness they won't leave you alone!" smiled Adam.

"Why are you smiling?" asked the student.

"Because many years ago I asked someone similar questions."

"And were the answers satisfactory?"

"All that I am now is because of the answers I got," said Adam, looking down as he thought about that life-changing conversation with the performer, which seemed so long ago.

"Before you leave, what final advice would you give me?" the student asked.

Adam paused a little, then smiled and said with a wink: "Find your hummus... it will set you free."

Recipe Book

Every person is perfectly designed to reach, enjoy and share their fullest potential. There are no excuses for an unfulfilled life.

It is never too late to be the beauty in other people's lives.

A few weeks later, on a pleasant evening, Adam saw a crowd gathering near one of his restaurants. As he walked into the crowd, he saw a familiar face. There he was, the street performer that Adam had met many years ago. Their old conversation came flooding back as if it were only yesterday.

"Do you remember me?" Adam asked the performer when he reached him, leaning forward with a smile.

"Sure do." The performer nodded and smiled back at him. "I often eat at your restaurants worldwide and I really love your hummus."

"I love to watch your performances on TV. They're always inspiring! I see that you kept in touch with the street." Adam looked around at the crowd.

"I never left," said the performer. "I see that you kept in touch with the street."

"I never left either," Adam said, shaking his head. A few seconds passed as they looked at each other, both thinking and smiling.

"Life is beautiful," Adam said.

"Life is beautiful." The performer nodded.

Adam started walking away, but then hesitated.

He turned to the performer.

"Hey," he said, "Do you have any plans later?"

The performer bent an arm behind his back and bowed playfully. "I'm flexible."

"We should travel the world," Adam said, "Drive country to country in a food truck, inspire others with our message."

"I'll cook and you'll entertain?" asked the performer with a sly smile.

"I was thinking the other way around," Adam laughed. "What do you say?"

The performer shrugged, "Let's do this shift."

After seeing the performer, Adam went for a walk. The sky was clear, and there was a refreshing breeze blowing in his face. It was all perfect, just as it should be. All around him were smiling faces and families enjoying their time. His attention then turned to a little boy a few meters away, flying a kite. In that moment, he remembered his young neighbor and laughed. He paused, and then whispered to himself, "I finally learned how to fly."

Recipe Book
Realistic is boring; be unrealistic.

Now it is
your turn to
find your HUMMUS

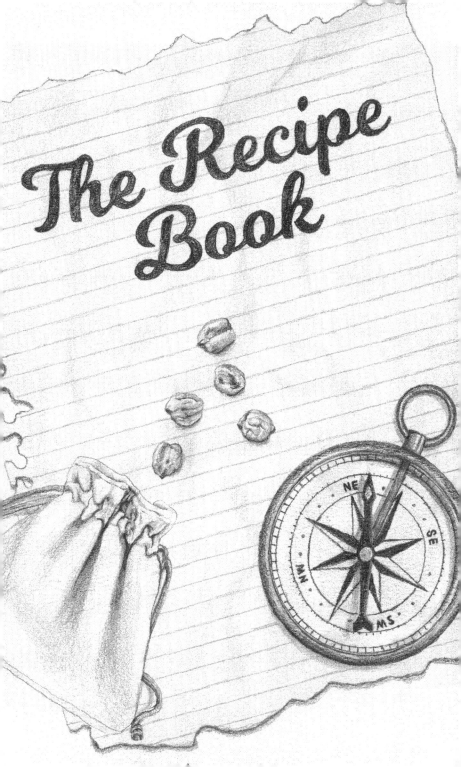

The recipe book insights along with questions are divided into sections. For example, if you would like to know yourself better, focus on the questions that relate to topics in the "Know Yourself" section. All of the questions and recipe books are placed into categories for your convenience.

You will have noticed that the three siblings from the Best family in the story you have just read all react and respond to the challenges they face differently from each other, according to their life experiences and unique perspectives. Each of us has responded to our own challenges in similar ways, at different stages of our journey of life.

Adam is usually open and adaptive to the changes of life, whereas Tom in contrast is rigid and blocks opportunities because of his frustration and fear of change. We see him repeatedly returning to his pattern of resistance, despite the pain it causes him. Even Adam at times feels discouraged and blocks his own progress. Sara is originally disoriented by the family's relocation, but begins to blossom and grow creatively.

Let us remind ourselves of some of the most significant realizations that each character had, during the period of their life which is illustrated in the story.

This is how each character is first introduced to us:

Adam:

"Adam read every cookery book in the house, and his creativity bloomed from their pages into the most wonderful shapes and tastes. He always carried around a notebook to jot down little notes for his recipes, but found that through cooking he often learned more about life than he had ever learned from a book." (Page 13)

Sara:

"Nights were hard for her because her haven that was once filled with her father's stories was now filled only with silence. She remembered the stories vividly and could conjure them into pictures in her head. She took to painting these pictures, charcoaling and inking and coloring paper to remember all the wonderful tales her Father had told her, and to drive back the silence that filled her head otherwise." (Pages 13-14)

Tom:

"The children didn't take the news too well, especially Tom, who was settled and happy in SOMELAND. He had met the perfect future wife for SOMELAND, but not for ANYLAND. She did not wish to leave, for she was content, and found changing life partners to be easier than changing life plans. At first, Tom considered staying, but as he was the eldest and the only one with work experience, he felt he needed to help his family out. He was driven by his sense of responsibility." (Page 14)

How would you describe each of these characters? Open or closed? Risk-taking and adventurous? Or risk-averse and cautious? Future-oriented and optimistic? Or locked in the past and fearful? Rigid and controlling or adaptive and expansive?

As you think about the questions in the section below, recall the incidents in the story in which the characters develop insight into themselves and the challenges they face.

Answer as many of the questions you can, and in the sections you prefer. They will give you great insights into your own thinking and that of your organizations.

Adam thoroughly reads his recipe book every month. He encourages that you do the same. The questions that you may wish to avoid answering are probably the most useful to you now. If the answers are not ready yet, take your time, but make sure you answer them... and that you find your Hummus.

CATEGORY I

Know Yourself

Everything Purpose Related

1. Living purposefully makes you shine.

What was the last thing you did that made you shine?

....

....

....

....

What was your company's most notable achievement?

....

....

....

....

2. Without a clear purpose, choices become reactive, resilience declines and life becomes harder.

What are you settling for?

....
....
....
....
....

In which areas of your life are you being reactive?

....
....
....
....

On reflection, which of your business decisions have been reactive, rather than purposeful?

....
....
....
....
....
....

3. Purpose does not have to sustain you financially. At the same time, it does not have to be charitable.

Are you working just to make money?

....
....
....
....
....

Do you experience fulfillment in your work?

....
....
....
....
....

How can you bring a deeper meaning to your paycheck?

....
....
....
....
....
....

4. Humans are designed to seek beyond basic survival. We are made for fulfillment.

ADAM: *"Going back to your point, it seems that lately, I've been so focused on just fighting for whatever job I can get that I forgot about what I truly love and what I'm good at." (Page 83)*

What is it that you do that makes you fulfilled?

....

....

....

....

....

5. Abundance and creativity make it possible to stay true to your special purpose, even when the surrounding environment changes.

SARA: *" She opened the door, and inside the room, paintings were hung on every inch of the walls. Paintings of SOMELAND, portraits of their family, memories that they had, and paintings of a future she imagined having in ANYLAND. They were beautiful and inspiring, lit up with the color of young enthusiasm, keen joy, and – perhaps most importantly – hope.*

Tom couldn't help but tear up. He was feeling so many things all at once. He was happy that his sister found a place for herself in ANYLAND by doing what she loved to do. At the same time, the paintings gave him a sense of her hope, which was almost like having some for himself. Through her eyes, he saw a visualization of how beautiful their life could be in ANYLAND, and a reminder of what it was like to be truly happy. (Page 57)

How are your core assets enriching you?

....
....
....
....
....
....

6. Purpose is about service. Service attracts love. Love heals wounds and leads to joy.

What problems can you help solve?

....
....
....
....
....

What opportunities are you creating?

....

....

....

....

....

7. Purpose is life's compass, it gives you direction.

To what extent can you attribute your problems to lack of purpose?

....

....

....

....

....

What areas in your life need more clarity?

....

....

....

....

....

....

....

In your business what unnecessary activities should you stop doing?

....
....
....
....
....
....

8. Purpose and passion are not the same. Passion is immense energy. Purpose is about using this energy to make life better for yourself and others.

How is your passion helping life get better?

....
....
....
....

What is your business passionate about-money at any cost or adding value to society? How?

....
....
....
....

9. You owe it to yourself to look within and find your purpose.

What is your purpose?

....
....
....
....

What is it that you do really well and how are you putting it in the service of others?

....
....
....
....
....

10. The biggest tragedy of your life is being aware of your purpose and not living it.

If your purpose is clear, why are you not living it?

....
....
....
....
....

Why is your life not aligned with your unique gifts?

....
....
....
....
....
....

11. Every person is perfectly designed to reach, enjoy and share their fullest potential. There are no excuses for an unfulfilled life.

How close are you to living your full potential?

....
....
....
....

In what way are you enjoying and sharing your true self and all that you've been given?

....
....
....
....
....

12. You were born to be your true self.

What does your true self look like?

....
....
....
....
....
....

What kind of person do you want to be?

....
....
....
....
....

What should you do today to become the best version of yourself?

....
....
....
....
....
....
....

13. Stay true to your purpose and life will take care of you

What strengthens your resilience?

....
....
....
....
....

How can you make your business more resilient?

....
....
....
....
....

14. We are designed to seek meaning. Without meaning the heart will know neither peace nor joy.

What brings meaning to your life?

....
....
....
....

What brings meaning to your organization?

....

....

....

....

....

....

Think of a time you felt was most meaningful in your life. Write it down. Remember it and seek it.

....

....

....

....

....

15. Purpose can manifest itself in many forms.

What are the different ways that you can express your uniqueness?

....

....

....

....

....

How can you translate your company's uniqueness into different forms of goods and services?

....

....

....

....

16. Questions to help you develop your purpose:

ADAM MEETS THE PERFORMER:
The performer pondered for a few seconds. "In the end, we all have to do what has to be done to survive. But I don't think that means we need to settle. I think there's always an abundance of opportunities, creativity, and resources to allow us to stay true to ourselves. The way I see it, our life isn't just about surviving, or losing our true selves to fit changing situations... that would be a kind of dying from the inside. Let me ask you this: what was the last job you had that you enjoyed?" (Page 81)

What can I do to make people seek me like they were seeking the performer?

....

....

....

What am I really good at?

....

....

....

....

What can I do to live according to my true self rather than just conform?

....

....

....

....

Am I doing what I truly want to do?

....

....

....

....

What is it that I can do that adds value to people so that they would gladly reward me with money, respect and admiration?

....

....

....

....

What would I do if I had no fears or responsibilities? What opportunities would I lose if I didn't try dreaming big?

....

....

....

....

....

How can I put my uniqueness in the service of others?

....

....

....

....

....

Emotions

1. Fear creates bondage. You are only free when you overcome your fears.

"Tom was mostly ruled by his fear. He had had a good life before, and he was scared, scared to start anew, so at any sign of trouble, he retreated back to his comfort zone: the past."(Page 67)

What fears are holding you back?

....
....
....
....
....

How can you break free?

....
....
....
....
....
....

2. Hope and abundance are everywhere. Self-pity is a destructive feeling.

What opportunities do you see around you, that you are hesitant about or scared of taking?

....
....
....
....

In what areas of your life do you tend to feel sorry for yourself?

....
....
....
....

3. Whatever hardship you face, someone has overcome something harder.

What challenges are overwhelming you, or your organization?

....
....
....
....
....

How did other people overcome similar challenges?

....
....
....
....
....

4. You can handle any situation in your life. Despair, blame, and self-pity are useless.

What challenges have you overcome in an inspiring way?

....
....
....
....
....
....

Mindset

1. Keep a child's fresh perspective on life. Remember when life was simple, you had beautiful dreams and you were curious and fearless.

What recently piqued your childlike curiosity?

....
....
....
....

What was the last lesson you learned from a child?

....
....
....
....

How can you describe your business and its value to a child?

....
....
....
....

2. You cannot build a better new reality with an outdated mindset.

What old ways of thinking do you feel are holding you back?

....
....
....
....
....
....

How can you replace your old ways with more useful ways?

....
....
....
....
....
....

3. Sometimes people escape to the past to avoid the challenges of the present, thus sacrificing the present and the future.

What are you avoiding?

....
....
....
....

In which areas of your life do you feel stuck?

....
....
....
....
....

Where is your company stuck?

....
....
....
....

What difficult business decision are you avoiding?

....
....
....
....
....
....

4. Every time you over-glorify the past as having been better, you're worsening a future that hasn't even had a chance to exist yet.

What past successes and failures are paralyzing you?

....
....
....
....

What past business successes or failures are you still dwelling upon?

....
....
....
....
....

What are you still holding onto that is not necessary?

....
....
....
....
....

5. Competition is a neverending battle. Only your uniqueness will shield you from it.

In what ways are you vulnerable to competition?

....

....

....

....

6. Without the first step, there is no journey to anywhere. Decide and act.

What first steps do you need to make to begin moving forward, to start something new, or to become unstuck?

....

....

....

....

How can you overcome what is preventing you from making the first step?

....

....

....

....

7. Don't compete. Create your own game.

Where in life are you being defensive?

....

....

....

....

In what areas of your business are you on the defense? How can you re-create the game?

....

....

....

....

....

8. You need to take care of yourself first so that you can take care of others.

How can you take better care of yourself?

....

....

....

....

....

....

In what ways have you ignored your own needs?

....
....
....
....
....
....
....

9. To always grow, always learn, always innovate.

When was the last time you invested in learning something new?

....
....
....
....

How are you keeping your skills polished?

....
....
....
....
....
....

10. Attitudes are contagious; make sure yours is worth catching. Positive attitudes inspire.

Remember Tom's negativity? He was not aware of how damaging its impact was: *"What opportunities?" asked Tom. "We're strangers here and we don't speak the language well. Besides, you're a farmer; so who is going to hire you in a city where there are no farming spaces? You're obsolete here, and there's nothing you can do."* (Page 24)

What is your dominant attitude?

....
....
....
....
....

How is it affecting others?

....
....
....
....
....
....
....

11. Being extraordinary means... Being more you!

Is your energy focused on being like others, or staying true to yourself?

....

....

....

Is your company still anchored in its original purpose for existence? If not, how far have you drifted and why?

....

....

....

....

12. You become the stories you tell yourself. You are the author of your own story.

What stories do you tell yourself?

....

....

....

....

....

How are your views limiting yourself and others?

....
....
....
....
....
....

What limiting view is holding your business back?

....
....
....
....
....
....

13. Realistic is boring; be unrealistic.

When was the last time you did something others might deem as crazy?

....
....
....
....
....
....

What can you do today to push the limits, something you would love to do, even it is not realistic?

....

....

....

....

....

CATEGORY II:

Know Others & Systems

Relationships and motivating others

1. Relationships are complicated and are loaded with obligations.

Can you deliver on the obligations of your relationships?

....
....
....
....
....
....
....
....

2. The people that you surround yourself with will shape your life. Embrace the positive and protect yourself from negativity, even if it comes from those closest to you.

Adam looked at his brother with mixed feelings of compassion and frustration. Many questions raced through his head about Tom: Why are you doing this to yourself and to people around you? Why are you so focused on your past wounds, not believing in your worth, in your ability to re-create yourself? Why are you selling yourself short, imprisoned by the fear of a fresh start? (Page 71)

Who uplifts you?

....
....
....
....

Who brings you down?

....
....
....
....
....

What poisonous relationships are you still holding on to?

....

....

....

....

Who is draining the energy of your organization?

....

....

....

....

What kind of culture are you actually rewarding?

....

....

....

....

3. You need to take care of yourself first so that you can take care of others.

Adam ceases to focus on Tom's problems and focuses on his own life: *"Although he was concerned for his brother, and sorry for his problems, Adam continued with his own life, helping Tom out whenever he saw an opportunity, and focusing on his own journey. He felt he had much to do in the world outside of his own family concerns, and needed to put his energy into it." (Page 115)*

How can you take better care of yourself?

....
....
....
....
....

In what ways have you ignored your own needs?

....
....
....
....

4. Every person is perfectly designed to reach, enjoy, and share thei fullest potential. There are no excuses for an unfulfilled life.

How close are you to living your full potential?

....
....
....
....

In what way are you enjoying and sharing your true self and all that you've been given?

....

....

....

....

....

....

5. It is never too late to be the beauty in other people's lives.

What false excuses have you been making for yourself to avoid living purposefully?

....

....

....

....

....

....

....

Business Focused

1. To build sustainable success, create raving customers who voluntarily promote the value of your purpose.

A week later, the menu of the restaurant was re- vamped with all of Adam's new dishes. The number of customers quickly increased, and waiting lists became a standard, first at weekends, then every night.

People, quite simply, loved Adam's cooking, especially the hummus. This exquisite dish was seasoned with herbs and spices similar to the ones he used to collect on the farm in SOMELAND. "More hummus" became a standard customer request. (Page 102)

Are you really making the customers your number one priority? How?

....

....

....

....

....

....

....

Are you creating customers who rave about you?

....

....

....

....

....

2. Always, always stay close to your customers.

In what ways are you listening to your customers' needs?

....

....

....

....

....

How can you meet their needs further?

....

....

....

....

....

....

....

Conflict and judging others

1. Never be quick to judge, surprises might be just a step away. Look beneath the surface.

Adam is taught by an old man how to fix a problem he could not solve himself:

Then the old man did something that Adam would never have expected. He let go of the cane and struggled for a moment to find his balance, but then bent down and plucked the wrench from Adam's hand. It took him only 10 minutes to fix a problem that Adam had been struggling with for over an hour. As the old man was getting up, he said, "You didn't expect that from an old man, did you? When you underestimate others, you only put limits on yourself. (Page 37)

When was the last time you were too quick to judge?

....
....
....
....
....
....

How did you change your mind?

....

....

....

....

2. Sacrifices should be made wisely and only when necessary.

Which sacrifices left you bitter and resentful?

....

....

....

....

3. Conflict is a scary sacrifice of peace. If it is necessary do not avoid it, but be selective, be prepared, and be strong.

Which necessary conflicts have you been running from?

....

....

....

....

....

What battles are you unnecessarily fighting?

....
....
....
....
....

4. If you can't change a reality, either leave or adapt to make the best of it.

What reality that you cannot change do you continue to complain about?

....
....
....
....
....
....

Why are you not accepting and trying to make the best out of it? Why haven't you left?

....
....
....
....
....

What reality do you know you can change? Why
are you not doing so?

....

....

....

....

....

....

5. The future is unpredictable, always be prepared for unexpected shifts.

What signs of change are you failing to read in
your personal life and in your business?

....

....

....

....

....

....

....

....

....

Competition

1. Competition is a never-ending battle. Only your uniqueness will shield you from it.

In what way are you vulnerable to competition?

....
....
....
....

2. Don't compete. Create your own game.

Where in life are you being defensive?

....
....
....
....

In what areas of your business are you on the defense?

....
....
....
....

How can you re-create the game?

....

....

....

....

....

3. Uniqueness neutralizes competition. Innovation maintains your uniqueness.

What makes you unique?

....

....

....

....

....

....

How does your uniqueness make competition irrelevant?

....

....

....

....

....

....

What is your business particularly good at?

....

....

....

....

4. Competition is about win-lose. It is focused on taking away your current and future opportunities.

Who are you competing with and why?

....

....

....

....

....

....

How would you describe your current role?

....

....

....

....

....

....

....

Does it build on your strengths?

....
....
....
....
....
....
....

CATEGORY III:

Leadership Skills

1. Be prepared: life is always changing and sometimes hard... Shift happens!

What were the biggest shifts in your life?

....
....
....
....
....

What were the biggest shifts in your business?

....
....
....
....
....
....

How does the culture of your company deal with external/internal changes?

....

....

....

....

2. Easy is not an option in life.

What is your default reaction to the challenges of life?

....

....

....

....

3. People are instinctively driven to survive and grow.

How much of your life is about survival versus growth?

....

....

....

....

....

4. You must remain intelligently adaptive, otherwise you will perish!

On a scale of 1 to 10, how would you rate your growth in life? In business?

....
....
....

How are you adapting to your current challenges and changes?

....
....
....
....
....

5. Arrogance prevents adaptation. Attitude and action that do not promote survival, lead to extinction. Arrogance can kill you.

In what situation did your ego ever stop you from moving forward?

....
....
....

Where in your business has arrogance and overconfidence led you astray?

....
....
....
....
....

6. Learning requires humility.

When has arrogance blocked your learning?

....
....
....
....

7. Adaptation is not easy. It requires courage, flexibility, experimentation, risk-taking, and hope for a brighter future.

Which areas of your life and business do you feel are too rigid?

....
....
....
....

How can you become more flexible?

....
....
....
....
....

What opportunities are you missing?

....
....
....
....
....
....

8. Don't compete. Create your own game.

Where in life are you being defensive?

....
....
....
....
....
....
....
....

In what areas of your business are you on the defensive?

....

....

....

....

....

How can you re-create the game?

....

....

....

....

9. Before you jump to the other side, make sure the greener grass there is not fake. Often our greatest growth opportunity is where we are now.

What can you do to fully explore all the opportunities that are now around you?

....

....

....

....

....

10. Change and uncertainty are natural processes; make them your friends.

How do you deal with change and uncertainty?

....
....
....
....
....
....

What are the reasons behind the change?

....
....
....
....
....

How can you turn uncertainty into opportunity?

....
....
....
....
....
....

11. Voluntary change should only be initiated when it is necessary or purposeful.

What kind of change should you introduce to further your growth?

....
....
....
....
....
....
....

12. Change by itself is just a process, not a purpose.

How are the current changes in your life helping you move forward?

....
....
....
....
....
....
....

What are the current changes in your life that are unnecessary? And in your business?

....
....
....
....

13. You need strategy and execution to transform your purpose into action.

In what way is your strategy a reflection of your purpose?

....
....
....
....

What is the quality of your execution?

....
....
....
....
....
....
....

14. The key to survival and growth is clarity of purpose and adaptability to change.

Remember, purpose doesn't change, circumstances do. Can you think of a time you changed the way things were done, but without changing why they were done?

....

....

....

....

....

....

The Author

Michael Kouly began his career as a Reuters war journalist. He covered armed conflicts that involved, Israel, Lebanon, Syria, Iran, Hezbullah, Islamic extremists, terrorism, the United States, Kuwait, Iraq and others... He also covered musical concerts, fashion shows and car racing.

Writing about wars, geopolitics, international diplomacy, and global events offered Michael unique opportunities to witness, analyze and write about leadership at the highest levels where bad leadership meant the loss of thousands of lives and good leadership led to avoiding wars, saving lives and rebuilding shattered countries.

Michael also exercised corporate leadership over a period of 30 years as he led the growth of regional and international businesses. He is a three-time CEO and president at organizations like Reuters, Orbit and Cambridge Institute for Global Leadership, managing people in more than 20 countries.

Over the span of his career, Michael made some good decisions that generated remarkable success and also some not so good decisions that offered valuable lessons on what works and what doesn't when exercising leadership - emphasizing the mindset of "you either win or learn".

From as far back as he can remember, Michael has been fascinated by leadership. He has spent his life learning about leadership, purpose and strategy by practicing them, watching others lead and by conducting extensive research on the art and science of mobilizing people and organizations towards growth and noble purposes.

Michael is a World Bank Fellow, author and keynote speaker about leadership, strategy, purpose and international politics. He is the founder of the Kouly Institute and the creator of unique Executive Leadership Programs, that have been delivered to thousands of top business executives, NGO and government leaders worldwide.

He also dedicates time to various non-profit organizations such as the Middle East Leadership Academy (MELA), Central Eurasia Leadership Academy (CELA), South East Asia Leadership Academy (SEALA) and Leaders Across Boarders (LAB).

His calling is to help people, organizations and countries lead purpose driven lives.

Michael studied at Harvard and Princeton Universities, and is an advisor to state leaders.

For comments, reviews and suggestions
contact Michael Kouly at
findingyourhummus@michaelkouly.com

Other Books By The Author

WIDE OPEN

Leadership is a dangerous enterprise, but the rewards are valuable. This book is designed to be your companion in your thrilling journey of remarkable survival and outstanding growth.

THIS UNIQUE AND ILLUMINATING BOOK WILL OPEN YOUR EYES WIDE, SO YOU LEARN MORE ABOUT:

- **Authority:** You are surrounded by authority figures such as parents, bosses, CEOs, presidents, or governments. As you already know, not understanding how to deal with authority is risky.

- **Enemies:** Enemies are a fact of life. They could be passive or aggressive. Enemies want to undermine you and your acts of leadership. Not understanding how to deal with enemies is dangerous.

- **Understanding Yourself and Others:** It is hard to survive and grow and to lead yourself without understanding what drives your thoughts, feelings, words, actions, behaviors, dreams, and ambitions. It is impossible to lead others without understanding them first.

- **Understanding Systems:** We live and work in systems. A system can be a family, team, company, community, city, country or the world. Systems have their unique psychology and rules. Not understanding systems will put your existence and progress at risk, as you may be excluded or isolated from the group that you belong to.

If I didn't Give A Sh*t I would...

As you will discover, this entertaining book of insightful and witty humor is not like other self help books.

WHILE ENJOYING THE EXPERIENCE OF THIS BOOK, YOU'LL ALSO:

- **Blow off steam:** We all have personal issues, challenges, and obstacles that accumulate stress that must be released to keep us in a state of peak motivation.

- **Know yourself:** Sometimes an entire life is spent being stuck at the expense of personal, business, social and relational opportunities for success. Self-discovery is the first step to the healing, actualization, and optimization of your life.

- **Reflect:** Recognizing your priorities, what you really want and what matters most to you is the key to your growth in all aspects of your life.

- **Decide:** To solve problems and catch opportunities, decisions are needed. This book will help you decide and act to expand your potential in a fun, playful, smart and effective way.

- **Lead:** True leadership starts with the self where smart and effective strategy, action and execution are the keys to the growth of our capacity.

In The Making...
A New Title
by Michael Kouly

Notes

Made in the USA
Middletown, DE
20 December 2018